THOTS ANONYMOUS

SHORT STORIES OF REAL THOTS

LORD SCUM BAG

LIT URBAN BOOKS

CONTENTS

By: LORD SCUM BAG

CHAPTER ONE INTRO

"Fuck me daddy fuck me" Alicia says, while pounding her pussy from behind Kalvin pulls on her hair and smack her ass nice and hard a couple times making her vagina cream even more. "Don't stop, please don't stop" she utters, "you like that dick baby" says Kalvin "Yes I looooove it she replies. Tell me you love that dick, yes daddy I love that dick, Kalvin smacks her juicy thick booty once more causing a shear shockwave of energy through her body, yea that's right, your daddy's little slut he whispers in her ear, almost instantly she starts to squirt and cum all over his cock, driving her crazy when he talks to her like that plus from the fast tempo and deep strokes she's receiving Kalvin did not climax yet so he tells her to turn back around to puts his dick back up in her wet pussy and begin stroking her nice and slow and then back stabbing her viciously like he was racing a 100 meters. 20mins later he finally reach his peak and pulled out and bust all over her apple bottom, she also came again at the same time. Her phone rings a couple minutes after they both climax and she answers hey baby, yea I'm just at work about to go lunch break, her husband calls her to say that he loves her. Yea Danny I'll be home around 4 30, I love you,.Kalvin then start to suck on her pussy for about an hour until her legs begin to shake and she came back to back several times. He pulls out of her and then tells her to turn around come taste your pussy. Like a obedient slave she turns around and devours his man wood and licks up every drop until the royal penis is clean.

CHAPTER 2 FACEBOOK TREESHA

It was just a regular summer day, with nothing to do the norm, 5pm as Kalvin grabs his time card and clocks out of work, tired and horny and frustrated with the same bullshit "thank you for calling Comcast cable how can I help you" must of been 90 or more irate customers pissed off because of the garbage, over charged billed, broken promises for troubleshooting issues and the list goes on, but he was glad to be off plus it was Friday aka pay day and he had a little pocket change to blow. As he goes to the check cashing store to cash his check he calls his weed man Fat boy aka Rashy Belly and pre-orders a dub (20) sack of mid grade weed and a (10) sack of loud aka Zaza, high grade or whatever the fuck you want to call it. He reaches the check cashing store and goes to cash his check 565$ for 2 weeks, smh (so much hell) he thinks to himself knowing he has to pay 475 worth on bill's. Left with 90 bucks to make it through the next 2 weeks and 30$ is already going to the weed man plus 17 dollars on alcohol Seagram's apple vodka aka the Ale, plus gas and food, he realize he's pretty much broke already but what the fuck, he was determined to enjoy his Friday and weekend. He pulls up to the Ptp palace which stands for pass the pussy and stops by Rashy Belly and grabs his herbal medicine, he knocks on the doors' he Rashy Belly opens the door,'was good nigga he says to Kalvin, ain't shit bro just leaving the plantation Kalvin responds. They head upstairs and converse about the weed he got and how it smokes, Rashy Belly told him to mix it because if you smoke the loud by itself you'll be stuck looking at the wall all day which was a good thing plus he knows Kalvin tolerance level was at a novice pace. Kalvin started to tell him about this fine Trinidadian chick he met on Facebook yesterday and she wanted to chill aka fuck tonight at least that's the mentality they have because they were a crew of friends Ptp Gooftroop affiliates were like bowling balls when it came to chicks, just going down the alley and making strikes all the time. Kalvin pulled up her page online and showed Bigga Ford, that bitch look nice, I bet you don't fuck tho he says the Kalvin, he responds you crazy as fuck she want to drink and smoke and chill at the beach, in Kalvins mind that's a 90% success rate of fucking he thought, females just don't want to drink and smoke with a random dude that they never met before unless they want some dick that's the mentality of a professional thot. They chopped it up some more before Kalvin gets back on the road and heads home. He reaches his destination around 6:15pm, walks upstairs to his apartment and relax. Immediately he starts the festivities, opened up a bottle of Seagram's vodka and begins to roll up a joint. Kalvin drinks like a sailor and is not that much of a smoker but he likes to indulge in his spare time and blend the weed with alcohol. He then started to text Treesha the fine thick booty Trinidadian chick from Facebook he met online the other day to see if she was still down to chill. She responds hey sexy how you doing, Kalvin replies I'm good just seeing was up with you and me for tonight. Yeah I should be ready around 9 o clock just got to finish up my homework and a few errands and I'll be ready, Ok cool, just hit me up when you're ready and send me the addy and I'll be on my way he says. Kalvin continues to drink and smoke half of the joint and then hops in the shower at 7 40pm. After a 25min shower he gets out and start getting ready, he kept it simple and dressed for the occasion, basketball shorts and a wife beater and Nike flip flops. He put on some smell good, splish splash everywhere, he was now a walking bottle of cologne, he went back to drinking and left the smoking alone for now so he can function properly. Treesha finally text she was ready around 8 45pm with address included Kalvin grabbed his bottle and a gram of the loud and regs and was on the way feeling saucy. He finally reaches her apartment and she invites him upstairs to meet her roommate country, perfect name for her because she was a super thick and country nice dark skin baby. He gave her a hug and grab her ass, he was in full thraug mode, and told her don't worry that's how I greet women when I first meet them, got to make sure ain't no lumps in your booty. She begins to laugh and says whatever nigga, you shot out. He thought to himself, she didn't slap me or show any resistance, I can fuck this bitch, but his eyes was on the prize, and focused on sexy ass Treesha. Thick thighs, smooth caramel skin, pretty curly hair, she smelt so good, like fruits and fragrances. He then gave Treesha a hug next and immediately grab her ass and licked on her neck, she just chuckled and gave off a little moan of ecstatic. Even though Kalvin had been drinking, his senses were sharp, very observant to her body and the effects his tongue had on her from just meeting her, he seen her nipples getting hard and goosebumps from his touch. His dick immediately got hard and he was already envisioning himself fucking and sucking her pussy, put he played it cool and went back into character. Treesha had on a bikini top and some tight ass booty shorts and bikini bottoms underneath, Damn baby you look so good, he complimented her, thank you she replied, baby girl you ready to go to the beach, yes I am. They finally left her apartment and got into Kalvin's car, a golds oldsmobile alero, nothing special a regular slider mobile. They were off to Fort Lauderdale beach, Kalvin pours a cup of vodka for himself, he always drinks and drive like it was legal, she ask if there's another cup, yeah he responds, in the bag. You got to pour your own poison though, she grabs the bag and makes her own cup and began to indulge into the festivities. Do you know how to roll, yeah a little, true well roll a joint while I drive, the blunt and weed is in the glove compartment. She grab the chocolate Dutch and split it down the middle and licked it like a champ and then broke down the weed and rolled the joint. Don't light it Kalvin told her, I don't smoke in the car wait till we get to the beach, they were having small talk the whole ride and drinking. He was looking at her thighs and his dick became brick, no questions ask he started rubbing on them and she was willing and glad for his touch, her eyes glared towards his crotch and saw the bulging print from his Johnson immediately her woman canal started to get moist from what she saw. Kalvin was use to turning a inch into a mile, so when she didn't stop him from rubbing her thighs he started rubbing her pussy through her shorts. He could feel the heat from her private area, causing his cod to jump repeatedly and she saw it, she let off a sensual moan and grabbed his wood through the shorts and then she went and pulled it out and started jacking on it as they drove closer towards the beach. They were almost there now looking for a parking space, both of them feeling good off the liquor both lustrous and yearning for each other in the worst way and both looking at each other like a snack ready to devour each other. They finally found a parking space on the side of the beach, she was still playing with his dick as he parked the car, he took a deep swig from his cup and then put down the windows and sparked up the joint. The first hit immediately was intense, he could feel the effects of that one pull plus the liquor intensify the feeling, his penis was so hard he could use it to cut a diamond, he took a few more puffs off the weed and then passed it to her, he was so ready for her, she grabbed the blunt and started smoking. She hit it 2 times and started coughing, her eyes were looking glossy but she was so horny and wanted to feel his dick inside of her, she hit the joint a few more times and then tried to pass it back to him but he refused, he knew his limits. He poured another cup and started sipping as she smoked the rest of the joint. Once finish they both agreed to walk on the beach, she wanted to get in the water but he didn't, but his brain, well his other brain down stairs started thinking for him and said fuck it, if the bitch want to get in the water I'm going in with her. As they walk on the shore the whole time his dick was on hard and she was rubbing on the dick while he was rubbing on her ass with his hands down her shorts and bikini, while kissing on her neck. They got to a spot on the beach close to the water where no one was there except for another couple at the top of the beach laying on a set of towels making out. They both didn't care neither did both couples, Kalvin and Treesha started kissing and tongue wrestling and rubbing on each other, she took off her shorts. Then she starts heading towards the water, Kalvin didn't want to get in the water but if that's where the pussy is going his dick said "get yo ass in that water and fuck that pussy", "sir yes sir!!" his body would reply and he followed her.

They both was now in the water waste deep, in his mind he was thinking of getting chewed up by sharks and risking it all for that juicy pussy. They started making out in the water, she wrapped her legs around him and he started grinding and poking at her hole through her bikini bottom, he slide her bottom to the side and slow pushed his rod inside of her. She let out a sexy moan as he pushed deeper inside of her. He was holding her up cuffing her from underneath her thighs. He started to work back and forth going balls deep with his 9 inch cock and she took it all, her walls felt decent but he could tell that the pussy had some mileage but it still felt good to him. It was hard for him to keep a good pace and thrust in and out of her because of the sand and the waves constantly knocking them over so they decided to get out the water and back by the shore. Once on the shore they continued to lust on one another, he laid in the sand near the water and she laid to the side started sucking on his salty balls and gagging herself on his penis, he was enjoying every minutes, after 5mins of her giving him head he flip her upside and started eating her pussy like a full course meal, her juice were dripping down his mouth and she was grinding on his face as he sucked and spit on her pussy, she was loving every bit of it and it was showing as she was returning the favor fucking his dick with her mouth and sucking the juices up and spitting all on the dick, they went at it for 15minutes then he got up and turned her around from behind and started fucking her doggy, straight raw the 2 was reckless not even asking for a condom from one another and gave too fucks, they were just in lust and enjoying the satisfaction.

Kalvin being the horn ball he is just couldn't resist, so the 2 thots went up top the lifeguard post. Treesha straddles on top of him and started to ride him like a bull. They were back at it sexing on the beach, people was walking by and watching and rooting them on and cheering, they didn't stop what they were doing, Treesha found it quite exhilarating and she became even more arose by the fact that she now had a audience and riding his dick.......After a few minutes the perverted bystanders finally went along with there day while Kalvin continued to hold on for his life on top of the lifeguard post and she was bouncing up and down on him. They both finally climax after 15mins of fucking. They were drenched in sweat and exhausted and both decided to leave the beach. Once back in the car they rolled up another joint for the ride, Kalvin I really enjoyed myself with you tonight she said, yeah me too, you got some good pussy and your a freak he replied, she started to laugh and said that's nothing, me and my roommate Ms. Cornbread we done did some real freaky ass shit, Kalvin saw that as a alley for her to bring that up to him and he was about to grab that shit like Shaquille O'Neal in his prime and dunk that bitch and break the goal. Oh yeah shit was up we should all link up me you Ms. Cornbread and I'll bring my cousin Toni, what he look like she asked??? After showing her a picture of Toni, her clitoris jumped and she responded uuuhh yeah I like him I'm down, I just got to run it by my friend Ms. Cornbread fed and see what she say, sometimes she be fronting and shit all depends what mood she in, she be tied up with her old sugar daddy she laughs and says. They was heading back to Treesha apartment to drop her off, they finished smoking the joint and Kalvin was back on hard from the weed and she started jawing him off while he was driving. They finally pulled up in the parking lot of her apartment, she continued to give him head and he busted in her mouth and she drained any bit of life he had left in him. Damn girl you a champ he said, she just smile and got out the car, he put down his window and said oh yeah I'm down for the orgy shitttt let me, I bet you are nasty self she said and laugh and went upstairs.

CHAPTER 3
BLIND CHICK

You got the Miami Raven you got some minutes to blow, blow with us he heard through the phone receiver, yessss Kalvin said out loud, I finally got on after trying for 20 minutes straight, the Miami Raven was a famous chat line back in the days, fill with all types of from, punks, crazy people, trannies, fat girls, weirdos, fine girls, thots which where bout its which evolved into thots through time and more. Once its night time its damn Near impossible to get on cause the whole south Florida is trying to get on At the same time especially on the weekends after 12 where the real deal action lurks. It was a Friday night and Kalvin being the thot he is was trying to find some action like a eskimo at a frozen pod with a pole and cut out ice cap waiting for a bite, He was over at his homeboy crib, El Niño aka pimp Chico, every one just hanging out with nothing to do, it was smiley the oldest, el Niño, Fat Boy Rashy Belly and Pooh Diddy, they we playing videos games mean while Kalvin was in the room trying to find a mission or pussy off the chatline, he was diligently working but didn't find anything after 20mins. He handed over the phone to pimp Chico and he was working his magic. Within a few minutes he found a girl who wanted to chill so they exchanged numbers and decided to get off the chatline and began to talk regular on the phone. They were doing the ol small talk where your from, what school you go to, how you look thing, like a job interview except it was to fuck. She said she goes to Boyd Anderson high school, she was short, dark skin nice curves and that he will like what he sees when he see her. Everything sounded good to el Niño but she said something that made him think for a little bit, she said that something was wrong with her eyes, at first he didn't think anything about it but he questioned her and ask her like what you mean by something wrong with your eyes...oh thing serious I just had eye surgery when I was young and my pupils are kind of white but I can see good in the dark, her answer seemed very strange and he started to question if she was blind. He told all the boys about what she said and smiley also went to Boyd Anderson and when he heard what she said to pimp Chico he thought about this blind chick that went to his school, the description was similar to this blind chick he knew from school but no way it could be her that's what he thought. After conversing for a half an hour, they started talking about sex and she was telling him she was a freak and that she love fucking and wanted to see him. So they agreed to link up, he told her that he didn't drive and his cousin was gone bring him to her condo and she was cool with it, so they all got ready and hopped in smiley car because he was the only one who drove at the time. They stop at the Walgreens and grabbed condoms and was heading to her place. While on the way they were reevaluating the conversation and making fun of pimp Chico by saying that she gone be blind and fat. After a 20 minute drive they finally reached the destination, they didn't have cell phones so once they got there el Nino got out the car and went up to the condo and knocked on the door, she opened up and it was dark in the house. She looked pretty decent body wise and she explained herself to a tee except for her eyes. He couldn't see her face because it was so dark, she led him upstairs and her brother was in the living room watching tv, they acknowledged each other and said was up then el Nino and girl went outside to the balcony. El Niño was kind of nervous for the fact her brother was outside and he didn't know what was he to think of a stranger in there house with intentions of smashing his sister, but he played it cool like nothing was bothering him, the chick started to ask him what's wrong, you don't like me or something?? He responded you straight but what's wrong with your eyes why they look like that, he was very blunt and never shy to hold back whatever on his mind. She says I'm blind, I hope that's ok with you, just that minute he began to think of smiley, Rashy Belly, Kalvin and Pooh Diddy the Haitian sensation and how they are going to make fun of him and roast him with jokes for what is happening, he responded to be honest I don't know what to think about this, I never been in a situation like this before. She understood where he was coming from and she said okay, then she said I guess you don't want no head or pussy then, he responded I don't know give me a few to think about it and i'm gone go by the car to let my cousin know i'm fine. Okay pimp Chico, he then responded what if my cousin want to fuck? She said okay that's cool, that fast he went to spread the word faster than Jesus disciples to the crew. He got to the car and everyone was so anxious to hear the story, so whats up bro? Pooh Diddy asked, bra she blind, nah you lying, nah bro I think it's the same girl smiley was talking about from school. They all bust out laughing from the coincidence of it being her, I told you smiley said. El Niño then said she wanted to fuck but I couldn't do it, out of the click el Niño was the boujee one, he had every right to be because he always had bad bitches or up to standard women since middle school. I told her my cousin might want in and she was cool with it, every was hyped from hearing that, like piranhas smelling blood in the water from a bleeding bird in a tree about to fall in the water as prey. Kalvin asked how she looked? He responded her body decent but that face and eyes tho, I couldn't do it. Kalvin immediately said I want in, then followed by me too from Bigga Ford. They decided to head back upstairs see for themselves. Rashy Belly, Kalvin and Pimp Chico went upstairs and she was now in the living room. Pimp Chico introduced them to her and the 2 vultures stared at the freshly carcass ready to feast, they didn't care about her face or eyes. They saw that body and realize she was ready to give up some pussy and was all in. Rashy Belly says so was up, she response you tell me, that's all the confirmation needed, Rashy Belly says let's go to the room, they all went in the room, she asked you got any condoms, yup right here and they all had condoms in hand. Kalvin Bigga Ford and blind chick all got on the bed. Kalvin pulled out his dick and she started reaching for his crotch area cause the bitch was blind but had senses like daredevil from marvel comics. She started working on Kalvin wood, he had the biggest smile and was enjoying her head, he wanted to laugh so bad but he keep his composure. She had all get clothes off and was actually sexy and petite, she was bent over in doggy position while giving head, Rashy Belly was behind her putting on a condom to fuck her from the back, he puts on the condom and starts thrusting back and forth for about 2-3 minutes, Kalvin was watching him and it looked weird because he was stroking his life away but it didn't look like he was inside of her, Rashy Belly started to say yeaaaa yeaaaa yeaaaa in his porno voice. Kalvin asked him aye are you in?? Rashy Belly responded yeah I'm in, blind chick responded no your not, el Niño and Kalvin erupted in laughter. After a few seconds from there he finally gets inside her and was pounding her doggy style while she was giving head to Kalvin, they were young kings 14-16 of age only smiley was 17 out of the group and blind chick was 18 too. inexperienced they were but bold and horny was all they needed to figure it out, after 10min they switched up, and laid on her back and Kalvin fucked her missionary while she was getting her face fucked by Rashy Belly. After another 10 minutes Kalvin came first then he got up and put on his clothes and went back to the car and told Pooh Diddy and Smiley what was going on, that fast they wanted in too, so they all went back upstairs and Smiley and Pooh Diddy joined in. First Rashy Belly and the Haitian sensation was getting head and then Bigga Ford finally came. Pooh Diddy was really enjoying the awesome head from her for about 30 minutes. Smiley was fucking her from the back and wanted to switch up but Pooh Diddy was stuck and couldn't get enough, quick fast quick fast quick fast he keep saying, that ended up being another 20 minutes. Smiley eventually came from fucking blind chick meanwhile Pooh Diddy was still getting head. He was the last one left and everyone started to head to the car, I'm almost finish yall boys, quick fast quick fast was the last thing they heard from him as they left and waited in the car. "Damn that nigga still ain't finish, 30 more minutes goes by and he still didn't come out yet," Kalvin says "I am gonna check on him maybe the brother got pissed off from us fucking his sister and kidnapped Pooh Diddy they all laughed. He walked back upstairs and Pooh Diddy still there getting head from blind chick. "You still don't bust yet?" ask Kalvin, "Nah bro I'm almost finished 10 more minutes quick fast quick fast." Pooh Diddy. 10min surpass and still no Pooh exiting, Kalvin walks back into the room and he still was getting head. Pooh Diddy just gave up and realize that he was never gone cum. He put on his clothes and said bye to blind chick and finally went back to the car. Damn nigga what took you so long el Niño asked? I couldn't bust he says, did you bust? Nope but it was good though he said, how tall think the brother feel? You think he know we all smashed his sister? Idk i think he probably knows and just don't give a fuck to be honest. They drove back to Smiley house to play 007 Golden Eye for the rest of the night.

CHAPTER 4 FAT FAT

"Aye Hollywood you almost finish with the computer pimp?" Kalvin asked, yea give me a few more minutes let me check my notes right quick. Bored with nothing to do on a Saturday night, Kalvin wasn't tired but as usual wanted some pussy. Hollywood finally finished checking his notes online and then got off the computer. This was back in 2002 there wasn't no fancy android or iPhones just computer internet, no 4g, 5g etc, internet on cellphones were trash and took forever to browse the internet on. It was pretty late around 3 30am and Kalvin was on blackplanet trying to find some pussy. It was a few girls online and he was talking to a few but getting nowhere, one female hit him up from a page that said deepthroat queen, it was a fat black chick looked very huge but he didn't care he was testosterone out and sexually driven and saw pass all that blubber out belly in her pics. They chatted on the instant message and exchanged numbers. They were texting back and forth and she decided to invite him over and wanted to suck his dick. He was down to ride, she lived in Pompano, he found it kind of odd that this bitch was so willing and ready to invite him over so late and was gone suck his dick but he thought to him self that that's the nature of sluts, no different from him, they want what they want. He hopped in the shower to get fresh then head out. Aye Hollywood I got a mission in Pompano, if I don't come back you know what happened he said and laughed. He called her before he left just to make sure she was awake, hello she answered, what's good what you got going, shit waiting on you to come over, she said, her voice sounded kind of weird to him, every time she talked it sounded like 3 voices at once, it was crazy to him, he asked her your a female right? Yes I'm a female, okay just checking, I'm about to start heading your way, ok see you soon, call me when you're outside. His other friend was in the other room Gorilla G and Kalvin went and told him about the 3 voice creature named Fat Fat and he wanted to ride with him so they both went on that ride. Kalvin and Gorilla G was off and on the way to pompano about a 20min drive, discussing the whole thing and Gorilla G wanted in too, try to see if she down for the train braa Gorilla G asked him, yea I got you ima ask when I'm there. They got off the exit Sample road from I-95 and pull up to these apartments near the exit, Kalvin started to get nervous because of the time frame and the location but he thought to himself I ain't got shit I'm broke robbing me and you gone be one pissed off motherfucker. He pulls up to the apartments and calls, it answered hello... what's good im outside Kalvin replies, okay I'm in apartment 106, ok I'm on my way and Kalvin hangs up. If I ain't out in 30mins I'm in apartment 106 he tells Gorilla G. He steps out and walks up to the apartment and knocks on the door. The door opens it was this huge offensive pulling guard that looks like she should be playing for the Miami Dolphins at the door, standing about 6 1 at least 300lbs. Kalvin walks inside the apartment, it smells like bacon, ass, and ball juice, he looks around it's not much furniture in the apartment a big screen tv, a couch and stereo set, reminds him of a traphouse. The creature walks towards her room and tells him to follow and he did. Once in the room there was no small talk what so ever, the creature said are you ready for this fire ass head and Kalvin pulled down his pants and it went to work on him, 5 minutes or less that boy was outta there K.O, she ate him up like a starving Somalian eating from Popeyes chicken.

After he bus, the creature went to the bathroom and got a warm rag and clean him up like a baby and then asked him if he wanted some more, the perverse demon in Kalvin said yes and the monster began to give intense CPR on his Johnson once more and again he exploded this time in 10 minutes. After the second nut he felt filthy and wanted to get away from the creature Fat Fat and he left, before leaving the creature said if you got any friends you can give them my number and immediately Kalvin told it that I have a friend outside that wants some and the thing told Kalvin to tell him to come inside. Kalvin finally leaves and was lost for words and confused because of what just went down but he couldn't lie those 2 nuts was intense, he gets back to the car and Gorilla G was excited to hear what happened in there with Fat Fat, Kalvin told him the run down on his experience and warned him of the apartment, how the creature look, etc and Gorilla G didn't budge one bit, he was ready to walk his horny ass in there and get his turn. He steps out the car and walks up to the apartment and knocks on the door, Fat Fat opens the door and Gorilla G was disappointed but still didn't care, he knew he was gone get what he came for and that's what he wanted. They greeted each other and she did the same thing, escorted her second victim to her room and like a hungry lion devoured his prey. Gorilla G was hooked, he also went for his seconds and she treated him the same. After he was finished she clean him up and sent him about his way and also told him to make sure you tell your friends. Gorilla G walked out 5 pounds lighter and had a giant smile on his face as he came back to the car. Damn brah that head was awesome he said to Kalvin, man I want to go back tomorrow grizzly said as they drove off to head back to Lauderhill. Kalvin felt different about going back, he had his fare share and was done, but not grizzly, for him it was just the beginning.

CHAPTER 5 HOES AT THE HAMPTON INN

On a hot summer night in Fort Lauderdale Kalvin and a group of friends were hanging out at the Hampton inn enjoying three Saturdays night. They had 3 rooms, it was 4 sluts(thots) Cece, Hawaii, Chico(Spanish girl) and Pinky and Kalvin, and uncle T. It was around 1am and every one wanted to have some fun that night so they all thought it was a good idea to get high on drugs and have a orgy. Everyone wanted to get on ecstasy, so fuck it that was the plan. Uncle Teezy called up his homeboy from pompano and ordered up a bunch of pills, blue and white hyenas and purple, red and green monkeys were the name of the pills. They went to pompano to pick them up and they' ended up grabbing about 20 pills. And a half of ounce of loud. After that they was off to the liquor store to grab 2 bottles of liquor and cigar wraps then back to the hotel. Kalvin ended up calling 2 more of his friends to join the party, Toni and Donavan, and told them to meet at the hotel. Uncle T went and dropped off the party accessories to the girls room and they immediately started to indulge into the drugs and liquor. Kalvin popped a blue hyena and uncle T took a white hyena. 10 minutes after taking the pills the drug was kicking in, they started to feel like Bruce Banner or Dr. Jekyll transforming into hulk and Mr. Hyde. They was waiting on Toni and Donovan in one of the rooms, they was high as fuck grinding on the side of there jaw and blowing like a tug boat, talking fast as fuck and at the end of every sentence was ya feel me, wshhhh. Donavan and Toni finally reached the hotel and Kalvin told them that its 4 girls in the other room getting high and drunk on drugs, they started to rub there hands like its time to feast on some pussy. They didn't take any drugs but they started drinking and was sauced out from the liquor. Theses 2 guys where animals when on liquor, young handsome and in great shape and fuck like jack rabbits it was a bad idea to bring your girlfriend or wife around them, they already had a out spoken personality but with liquor just made them even bolder and aggressive and the bitches loved it and they knew it and that's what made it worst they were sharp. When it came to women they were sharp. In the other room was 4 girls high and out of there minds, God knows what was going through there minds at the time, clitoris and vaginal walls probably was jumping up and down and raging for a good hard pounding and little did they know that it stood 20 feet down the hall from them.

The guys decided to take a trip to the girls room. Once they entered they all noticed how high the girls was. Hawaii laying on her back on the bed looking at the ceiling and keep saying I'm high as fuck, I cant move, Cece was high but she was quiet and just sitting on the other bed and looking around in the room, Chico was so high she was just looking at her phone, her cellphone rigged and she ended up picking up the room phone instead and start saying hello and trying to talk to someone but she didn't even realize that she answered the wrong phone. Pinkie was high but not high enough, she ended up taking 3 pills but still wasn't high like the 3 other girls, she was used to smoking hard or crack so I guess taking ecstasy was a notch down for her.

The guys were all horn balls naturally but at this point from being intoxicated and being on drugs made it worst for them, they all went for there victim, Kalvin and Toni went for Cece, Uncle Teezy went for Chico and Donavan went for Hawaii, nobody really wanted pinkie, she was pretty black and Spanish mixed but she was a big block so she was last priority, Kalvin started to get head from Cece while Toni started fucking her from the back, Cece pussy was so wet and always stay wet, she had the super soka, Donavan was getting head from Hawaii, Donovan has 3 legs he was well endowed and was a energizer bunny she had it coming to her. Chico was so high, she wanted to enjoy herself but she was in a different mind state at times, uncle T brought her in the bathroom and bent her over on the bathroom sink and started to give her a pounding. Every one started to switch up, Kalvin went to Hawaii, Donovan went to Cece, Toni gave Pinky sympathy dick and uncle Teezy keep at it in the bathroom with Chico, the fuck fest lasted about 3 hours of switching and fucking, after a while everyone died out except Donavan, once he got his turn at Cece they she stuck in each other like 2 dogs in heat for breeding, her pussy never got dry not once, her juices were slippery and always leaking and her walls weren't worn out, she was young and loved dick, she even eat Chico pussy that night. They went from the bed, to the shower, Donavon had work at 5 in the morning all the way in Homestead Florida that morning, if it wasn't for work he probably would of been fucking her for another few hours, he dropped Toni home and went to work and Uncle Teezy and Kalvin went to there rooms and fell asleep, the girls all eventually all passed out and ended there night.

CHAPTER 6 KIKI ORLANDO

***First time taking drugs. Ecstasy

Just another day in the life of a thot, Kalvin was traveling to Central Florida Haines City to be exact to visit family for summer vacation from college. Haines City is a small city and really nothing to do there he thought to himself plus he didn't know anyone in the area. He was tired of being stuck in the house with nothing to do so he decided to get online to see if he could meet any females from off blackplanet. Indeed he found someone, this beautiful island woman name Kiki from Orlando, she was a older woman around 33, he was 21 at the time. They started to converse online and later exchanged numbers. Through out the week they planned on meeting up on a Friday, first meeting at Winghouse which was a bootleg hooters restaurant for food and drinks and getting to know each other in person and if the vibe was right they would go back to her condo.

There out there weekly conversation they would talk about the normal things to get to know each other then she started asking him if he drink and smoke weed, at the time Kalvin did smoke and drink but not much, then Kiki ask if he pop off aka do you take pills or beans which they were called, Kalvin responded that he didn't but he thought about trying it. Kiki was a older experienced women and was very confident with her sexuality and the things she did and told him that she takes ecstasy and would tell him about her experience and how it made her feel, Kalvin bit the bait and she was reeling him in to take pills with her so she can basically turn his spring chicken ass out. The things were enticing him and curiosity kills the cat, so they planned to get high on drugs together if there pre meet and greet worked out good.

Friday finally comes along and they planned to get together after she got off work. They planned to meet up at 7 o clock at the Winghouse restaurant. Kiki got off at 5 o clock from her job and texted her victim aka Kalvin telling him she was heading home to get herself together and confirm there meet up at 7. Kalvin started to get ready and hopped in the shower and threw on his clothes and head out. He threw on his like green Lacoste dress shirt and khaki shorts and casual timberland booths and was on the road. He stopped at a liquor store and grabbed a bottle of vodka for when they chilled at her place. She had already pre-ordered weed and pills from her dealer. It would take him about an hour or so to get there because of the distance and traffic on interstate 4. Kalvin was coming up to good exit off I-4 and Kirkman Rd and texted Kiki letting her know he was almost there and she was already there waiting and talking to her friend that works there she said, she will be inside waiting and she has on a black short dress skirt and white top heels. Kalvin finally arrived to his destination. He then calls her and let her know he is out side, she told him where she was sitting and she had ordered a couple drinks talking to her friend. Kalvin walks in the restaurants and met up with her where she said she was sitting and noticed this beautiful woman, dark skinned tone, long dreads, perky breasts, beautiful smile sitting at the table with one of the employees which was also beautiful, a young white tall blonde woman with nice titties and thighs. Kalvin walks up to the table and introduce himself to both women, how you beautiful ladies doing he says, well mannered he introduced himself to the waiter and gives her a hug, she smelled so eatable, hi Kalvin I'm Ashley Kiki's friend, he then gives Kiki's a warm hug and she too smelled delicious and had a nice tight body, she sat back down and Kalvin sat across from her. They begin to talk about there appearances with each other asking each other if they looked liked there pictures online and did they like what they say in person and both agreed that they did. They then ordered some wings and jug of beer and began dissecting each other physically and mentally To get a clear observation of each other, another fine young waitress brought out the food and brew and

Kiki's started to flirt with her when she arrived at the table, she was very aggressive and even grabbed on the waitress ass, the waitress was shy and started to blush by the attention she was getting from Kiki, come here with pure aggression and assurance like she owned this bitch and knew this girl her whole life Kiki says, the girl slowly comes closer to Kiki, she's grabs a handful of her juicy ass cheek and says I like you what's your name I never seen you here before are you new? Kiki asked her. She giggles like a 11 year old, ye ye yes she stuttered I'm new, my name is Brittany she says. Ok Brittany well I 'ma get your number before I leave Kiki says... okay Brittany respond and walks off. Kalvin watched the whole thing anyone didn't say a word, in his mind he was thinking wow what the fuck was that, this bitch aggressive of fuck and he liked it, he was used to a lot of different women but he never seen a woman just take another woman like that. He asked her that's how you doing it, with coincidence Kiki respond hell yeah, these bitches ain't shit, I come here all the time and I turn a lot of them out, they a bunch of good looking broke ass hoes just trying to get a check, yea I'm bisexual if you don't know by now, nah I couldn't tell sarcastically Kalvin responded.

They continued getting to know each other and ate for about 30minutes, then she said you ready to go back to my place, the sounds Kalvin was waiting for, he played it cool yea I'm ready, he got a doggy bag for wings cause them shits was good as fuck and

Kiki down her last mug of beer and they paid for the food and drinks and we're off, Kiki did went back for Brittany number like she promised, yea i'm gone fuck her soon she says when they walked out the restaurant Kiki says, I don't stay to far from here Kiki says follow me. She gets in her BMW 528 And Kalvin jumps in his Chevy Impala dope boy whip and starts to follow her back to her place. Kalvin was ready to fuck this bitch or so he thought at least, they drove about 10mins to her complex a nice gated condominium, she punched in the password and waves him in and then she droved in. He followed her and she pulled up to her 3 story condo and opened the garage and parks inside, Kalvin parked outside and walks in the garage. They walk upstairs together, she walks in front of him meanwhile he was looking up her skirt she had on no draws, he instantly got on hard from looking and thinking to himself that we bout to fuck. The second floor was the living room and kitchen, he didn't have much furniture in her place maybe she just moved here Kalvin thought, he really didn't give a fuck he wanted that fine ass bitch. She grabbed a bucket filled of ice for the bottle Kalvin picked up earlier. They went up to the 3rd floor which was her bed room, it was very nice and elegant, very thing was top scale and new from her bed, dresser, tv. Her closet was full with all types of clothes and shoes, she told him to make yourself comfortable, Kalvin sat on the bed kind of nervous, she went to her draw and pulled out some weed and 4 green ecstasy pills. Kalvin sits on the bed looking like curious George, what's that he asked, these are green monkeys the serpent responds as she rolls up a joint. Like what does it do or how it makes you feel, is it like weed? Or alcohol? The young fella asked her, nah it's like neither she responded, it has its own feeling like a euphoric type of vibe, you become sensitive to touch and emotions and everything is intensified 10x, conversation become more deeply, passion is expressed on another level it's kind of hard to explain it but you will feel what I'm talking about she says to Kalvin. She took 2 pills then broke both of them in half and told him to take half of one now and we gone take the other half later, they both popped half. She got up and said I'm gone take a shower and change into something more comfortable. He poured a cup of vodka and began drinking it straight and lit up the joint. He sat there on the bed and in 10 minutes he started to feel everything had intensified from his breathing and his thought process, he hit the joint a few times and went to the bathroom to pass the joint to Kiki in the shower, he gave her the joint and analyzed her naked body and how beautiful she was from head to toe, or should he say head to ankles cause he realized she had some big ass sideshow Bob feet but he didn't think much of it cause she was pretty, titties perfectly round which he realized she had fake breast and slim petite figure and pretty long dreads, she looked easily 19-21 years of age He grabbed the joint and went back on the bed, he took off his clothes and was in basketball shorts and took his shirt off, at this point the drug kicked in even higher mixed with the weed, the liquor became water at the moment and he started wash the vodka down like juice and it had no effect on him. Kiki finally came out the shower in a sexy black lingerie. Her pill had kicked in too but she was veteran and new what to expect and how to handle her high. Kalvin was talking a lot not normal for him, they started to have a passionate conversation about the littlest things like they were talking about her laptop and they really had a real conversation about it to the point they both realized that there talking about it for 30min just stupid shit was so amazing to discuss to them. They decided to take another half of the pill together, Kalvin brought his Wiz Khalifa cabin fever mixtape with him and put it on in her laptop. She hooked it up to speakers played it loud, the vibe intensified even more with music, something that Kalvin realized and then he keep asking her am I supposed to feel like this, how long am I gone feel like this, his eyes geeked out from the pill and his jaw grinding on teeth, she sat on his lap and started to reassure that he will be fine just relax and vibe, you gone be high for 3 to 6 hours, she didn't want him freaking out or anything because it was his first time rolling. He held his composure and just let her be in control.

A song called find me in the middle of you came on and it was like they both fell in another dimension, she was vibing off the music and dancing and Kalvin was just watching her as she captivated him with her sexual moves and when she touched his body it was intense. they started kissing each other and making out on the bed, intense for play both licking, sucking and touching teasing each other. Kalvin started to lick her neck, and suck on her sexy round hard fake titties, it was his first time seeing fake titts, to him they looked awesome but he gave 2 fucks for how they felt, there pretty much for show and white men liked them, Kalvin preferred real breast he realized but it wasn't a big deal he was enjoying the ride, He then started kissing her stomach down to her thighs, and she grabbed him by the back of his head and put his face on her pussy and started to grind on his mouth, he sucked on her clit like a pacifier and worked circles with his tongue as she grind harder and harder. He wanted to see how her head was so he stopped and laid on his back then flipped her upside down and went back to eating pussy, he became even more into eating her, he stuck his tongue inside her vagina and started fucking her with his tongue and she became even wetter. She started sucking on his dick while doing 69, she started out nice and sensual and then started giving nasty porno head as he started to please her more and more with his tongue, she gagged on his cock and spit on his dick and balls and started sucking on them. He grabbed her ass cheeks and spit on her pussy and was pulling her hips up and down and sucking her pussy, the sound was so exhilarating, sloppy spit and slurping and his rode his face and he just keep going. She was getting exactly what she wanted from him, turning this young buck out and enjoying every bit, Kalvin notice she keep trying to lower her body as she rode his face so that her asshole will fall right on his tongue and he keep pushing and putting resistance towards her so that she didn't move her asshole on his mouth. He never ate booty before and never thought of doing anything like that, didn't really appeal to him, she was very persistent on getting him to eat the groceries, she grabbed him by the back of the head so he couldn't move damn near smuttering him to death until yea got his ass, like breaking a bull, next thing you no Kalvin was eating ass and just keep on going, he then started fingering her in the butt, it turned her on. They went at it for 3 hours straight, he ended up fucking all 3 of her holes and cam in her ass and pussy, just str8 reckless. Some guy ended up calling her phone her ex and she was such a freak that she asked Kalvin if he can join so they both can fuck her but Kalvin wasn't bout that, for one he didn't know the dude and he was rolling off beans, he thought to his self what if this nigga touch me or try me I'ma kill this nigga, he ran plenty of trains so that's wasn't the problem, he just didn't know this nigga, and wasn't gone be around some random motherfucker on some shit like that, he mentioned to Kiki that good cousin lives in Orlando on the East side if you want a 3 some he'll slide through a and we can get it on. It was his dog Mel he was a Savage and a young pup that would slay her real nice, Kalvin called him up and have Kiki the phone so they can talk, she told him what was going on how they were fucking and he told her about his cousin, so she did her interview to see he was her type but she refused to go through with it, so they just left it alone. They went back at it for another round and Kalvin bust a juicy nut and his body just passed out. He woke up naked around 10am, to him only, she was gone no where in site, he started to panic. He went downstairs and checked the living room no site of her, he went to the garage her car was gone. He went back upstairs to the bedroom and looked out the window his car was still there parked to the side, he started to ask himself what happened, he could only recall certain moments throughout the night. He finally thought call her to see if she everything was ok. He called her and she picked up, hey what's up she answered, Kalvin asked her what happened, she said we was fucking all night and then we fell asleep, I got up early around 6 and been up since, I couldn't go back to sleep. Where are you Kalvin asked, I'm at Chipotle down the street, do you want something to eat? Yes chicken bowl he responded, ok come meet me up here, so Kalvin got up and put his clothes on and hoped in the car and started heading to Chipotle once there they meet up inside and ate and chatted about there experience together last night and how they both enjoyed each other's company and would do it again together in the near future, after they finished eating and chatting they went there separate ways and call it a day.